UNKNOWN SECRETS OF WORLD WAR II

MARK WROBEL

Unknown Secrets of World War II

By Mark Wrobel

Cover Created & Designed by Jazzy Kitty Publications

Logo Designs by Andre M. Saunders/Jess Zimmerman

Editor: Anelda L. Attaway

© 2021 Mark Wrobel

ISBN 978-1-954425-25-5

Library of Congress Control Number: 2021907990

All rights reserved. This book is protected by the copyright laws of the United States of America. This book may not be copied or reprinted for commercial gain or profit. The use of short quotations or occasional page copying for personal or group study is permitted and encouraged. Permission will be granted upon request. This book is for Worldwide Distribution and printed in the United States of America, published by Jazzy Kitty Publications utilizing Microsoft Publishing Software.

ACKNOWLEDGMENT

First and foremost, I acknowledge God and thank Him for sustaining me through life with my disability.

DEDICATION

I dedicate this book to my long time friend Rosemarie Arcaro.

TABLE OF CONTENTS

INTRODUCTION..i
CHAPTER 1 – The Nora Berg Laws of the 1930s…............................02
CHAPTER 2 – Who Was the Real Adolf Hitler 06
CHAPTER 3 – The Origins of the Organizations 10
CHAPTER 4 – The Origins of the German/Nazi Swastika.....................16
CHAPTER 5 – The Black and the Arab Soldiers of the Third Reich........21
CHAPTER 6 – Was the Aryan Race Real or Fake....................................25
CHAPTER 7 – The German Time Machine...31
CHAPTER 8 – The Holocaust Industry 34
CHAPTER 9 – The Escape of Adolf Hitler..39
CHAPTER 10 – The Vatican and the Third Reich................................... .44
CHAPTER 11 – Control of the Population Through Religion.................. .48
ABOUT THE AUTHOR 53
REFERENCES.. ..55

INTRODUCTION

I am writing this book because I want to discuss a piece of American/World History about World War II that no one has thoroughly examined.

I am not a historical revisionist, nor am I a member of the American right-wing. I am neither a supporter in no shape or form of fascist ideology either. I just want to take a closer look at a piece of World War II history that has not been looked at very much by mainstream historians.

ADOLF EICHMANN   **ERICH VON MANSTEIN**   **REINHARD HIDRICK**

ADOLF EICHMANN WAS ONE OF THE MOST NOTORIOUS MEMBERS OF THE SS AND HE CAME FROM A RICH JEWISH FAMILY

ERICH VON MANSTEIN WAS FROM A PROMINENT JEWISH FAMILY.

REINHARD HIDRICK WAS OF JEWISH DESCENT. HIS FATHER WAS A MUSIC COMPOSER, AND HIS MOTHER WAS A RICH ARISTOCRAT. BOTH WERE OF JEWISH DESCENT.

CHAPTER 1

The Nora Berg Laws of the 1930s (How they function in Practice)

Did you know that there were about 150,000 Jewish soldiers that served in the German army and the German SS between the years 1930 through 1945. I know you think that this is just a made-up story. Unfortunately, it is not; there were soldiers of Jewish descent that served in the German army during World War II. (NBC, 2020). To understand how this happened and how it worked, we have to take a closer look at the Nora Berg Laws.

1. If your father and mother were of Jewish descent, you could not join the German military.

2. If your mother was of Jewish descent, but your father was not, then you were obligated to serve under the German draft laws of 1930. The same thing applied if your mother was not of Jewish descent, but your father was.

3. If you were rich and could pay off the German officials, you could obtain an Aryan certificate from the Ministry of Culture, and then you could join the German army back in the 1930s. (Story, 2020)

One of the German officers of Jewish descent who served in the German army during World War II was Erhard Milch. He was an assistant secretary to the commander of the German Air Force Herman Goering in 1939. (2020) Another German officer of Jewish descent who also served in the German army during World War II was Erich Von Manstein. (2020) He was the chief planner of the invasion of Poland in September 1939. Many German soldiers of Jewish descent have served in the German army from the 1930s to 1945.

The other two names that I have to mention here are Adolf Eichmann and Reinhard Heidrick. (2020) (2020)

You might be asking questions:

How come when Germany had the Nora Berg Laws back in the 1930s?

How come all those men were able to join the German army?

Some of them did join the dreaded German SS because those people came from wealthy families. Therefore, they were able to bribe German officials. But, if you were a hard-working Jewish person back in the 1930s and you came from a low-income family (poor), then you were in big trouble.

You might be asking a question right about now, but history books say that the Nazis have killed about 6 million Jews. However, what you have to remember is that Jews are not the only ones who perished in the German concentration camps. Many people of European descent and the Gypsies have suffered under the German rule.

The biggest murderer of people was Reinhard Heidrick; he was of Jewish descent himself. He was the equivalent of a governor of Czechoslovakia in the late 30s and early 40s. He was responsible for the death of 5000 Jews in all of Czechoslovakia. (2020). His father was Richard Bruno Heydrich. He was a classical music composer, and his mother was a wealthy German aristocrat. Reinhard Heidrick came from a very privileged family, and yes, both of his parents were of Jewish background. (2020) So, as you can see, money holds power today, just as it did back then.

One other individual that is worth mentioning is Albert Spear, who was part of the Nazi party. He was the architect who helped Hitler and the

Nazi Party designed the building plans for their so-called Germany. Albert Spear might have been one of the wealthiest founders of the National Socialist Party of Germany, Nazi for short. He was also born into a wealthy, privileged family. And by trade, he was an architect. Most of the buildings in Germany today were redesigned by Albert Spear right after World War II and in 2020, right after World War II. (2020)

Adolf Hitler was born in a German village in Braunau Am Inn. Later, he turned that particular village into an artillery training center so that the German people would not find out the possibility of Adolf Hitler's family's Jewish origins. (Jerusalem Post, 2019) (2008)

CLARA SCHICKLGUBER   ALOIS SCHICKERGUBER

When Adolf's father got a job as an Austrian customs official/civil servant, he changed his name to Hitler before Adolf Hitler was born. Everything else about Adolf Hitler is true.

CHAPTER 2

Who Was the Real Adolf Hitler

Most things that you have learned in history books are controlled by the powers that be. However, when it comes to history, the truth sometimes is stranger than fiction. So, in this case, the history of the Second World War was also censored.

We all know that Germany's leader from the 1930s until 1945 was Adolf Hitler. However, did you know that Adolf Hitler is not his real name? His real name was Adolf Schicklgruber, his mother's name was Clara Schicklgruber and his father's name was Alois Schicklgruber. When Adolf's father got a job as an Austrian customs official/civil servant, he changed his name to Hitler before Adolf Hitler was born. Everything else about Adolf Hitler is true.

So how did Adolf Hitler come to power?

He came to power between the late 20s, early 30s? After World War I, he was sent by the German military to spy on the National Socialist Party's meetings that were getting started in Germany, in Bavaria, to be exact. He soon discovered that he had a talent for speaking well in public, so the people started to like what he had to say.

What you have to understand is when the Nazi Party was forming in the early 20s, Germany was going through a very bad economic depression. When Germany started to pay war reparations after World War I, Germany was in very heavy economic debt. However, you have to understand that two secret societies that backed Hitler's bid for power were called the Thule Society and the other called the Vril Society.

One more secret society that might have helped put Adolf Hitler in power is the Illuminati Secret Society. We will go in-depth to discuss further those particular secret societies in the next chapter.

Those organizations, such as Thule Society, Vril, and the Illuminati, are still with us today. They are the ones who are part of what we call Global Governance/The New World Order. Those organizations may be part of the Freemasons today.

Let me make something perfectly clear, yes, Adolf Hitler was a very evil man. However, in this book, I am trying to take you on the journey behind the scenes so that you can see that people like Adolf Hitler do not function in a vacuum. Those kinds of people are backed by billionaire organizations that have their own agendas.

Yes, Adolf Hitler did support what we call the Eugenics Program. If you are a person with a physical or mental disability, you are basically eliminated from society permanently. One other gentleman has also supported the idea of eugenics here in America, and his name was Henry Ford. Yes, the same Henry Ford that was the Ford Corporation owner who produces cars and trucks today. Henry Ford was not the only person who has supported the eugenics movement in America. One other person has supported the eugenics movement herself, and her name was Margaret Sanger. She might have been a member of one of the secret organizations that control what happens in our world today.

Those of you who have read my books understand that nothing happens in this world by chance; everything happens by design.

Those organizations that had supported the Third Reich in the early 30s through the 40s are still active today. Of course, they have changed their names and their location. However, they still promote the agenda of

Global Governance and World Domination.

The person who has first discovered the agenda that those organizations, like the Illuminati and the Freemasons and many others, was R. C. Christian. He wrote them down on the stones located in Georgia today. And yes, those that I have mentioned above have for humanity.

Those organizations, such as the Illuminati, the Thule Society, and the Vril Society, are responsible for creating the European Union and its structure. Those particular organizations still exist except under different names.

DR. VON BRAUN DR. HANS KAMMLER

DR. VON BRAUN & DR. HANS KAMMLER BOTH HAVE BEEN MEMBERS OF THE VRIL SOCIETY

CHAPTER 3

The Origins of the Organizations - Who Put Hitler in Power?

The first organization that put Hitler in power was the Thule Society. The Thule Society was founded in Germany in 1918. This particular organization has funded Hitler's rise to power.

The founder of the Thule Society was a wealthy German aristocrat named Adam Alfred Rudolf Glauer, also known as Rudolf Freiherr von Sebottendorff (von Sebottendorf 2020). The leader of this particular organization was Walter Nauhaus; he was another wealthy German aristocrat.

You have to understand that many wealthy people included the German rich Jewish aristocrats, have messed around with what we call de--occult studies back in those days. Although Adolf Hitler himself was raised in a strictly Catholic family, he was not a Christian. His beliefs were based on paganism and Slavic/ancient beliefs.

Another secret society that put Adolf Hitler into power back in the late 20s and early 30s was called the Vril Society. This particular society was interested in researching space and time travel technology. One of its members was Alfred Rosenberg. (2021) He was one of the Vril Society founders, just as the Thule Society was the financial backers of the National Socialist Party in Germany back in the 1920s and 30s. The Vril Society was also backing the Nazi Party financially. However, they were more interested in space and time travel technology. There is speculation that the Vril Society has invented the Time Machine back in the 1940s in Poland. (2001)

Yes, the financial backing of the Nazi Party itself was done by the two-secret society. One of them was called the Thule Society, and the other secret society was called the Vril Society. The Thule Society handled the financial side of the Nazi Party. The Vril Society dealt with the technical side of things. You see, the Vril Society itself was composed of engineers and other people with the necessary, scientific, and technical backgrounds. However, the Vril Society itself wasn't able to secure some funding on its own from different sources. The members of the Vril Society might have been people like Dr. Von Braun and Dr. Hans Kammler. Whether this time travel technology worked, we will get into this in the next couple of chapters.

The last secret society that might have backed Hitler's bid for power back in the early 1920s and the 1930s in Germany was a secret society called the Illuminati.

Is the secret society of the Illuminati real or fake?

In my opinion, the secret society of the Illuminati is real and it still exists today. The Illuminati was founded on May 1, 1748, in Bavaria, Germany, by a German aristocrat named Adam Weishaupt. Adam Weishaupt (1748–1830), believe it or not, these are the people who still run the European and world affairs to this day, with the cooperation of other secret societies, like the Freemasons. The Illuminati themselves might have been responsible for the financial support of Adolf Hitler so that he could have been put into power. (2020)

In reality, the third Reich has never ended. However, that third Reich was transformed into the real European Union that the Illuminati and another secret society rule. There are about 12 of them; one of the groups that might have helped in this endeavor is the Majestic 12. President

Dwight D. Eisenhower was aware of this back in the late 40s and early 50s.

Those organizations such as the Freemasons, the Illuminati, and many others, still control our financial system to this very day. In my opinion, those organizations and the power that they hold all over the world are very strong. How strong? Those particular organizations, in my opinion, may even have the power to manipulate our election system in America. That is the biggest security threat, in my opinion, to a republic. I can and will give you evidence of how this might be accomplished. (Norton, 2020) We don't even know what happened to one of the Vril Society members, Dr. Hans Kammler, to this very day.

The next question that we should be asking ourselves did the Nazi in World War II possess a prototype of a working Time Machine itself? We will discuss this in the next couple of chapters because the German Time Machine story is really fascinating.

The other part of this piece of history that we are, examining in this particular book is that the National Socialist Party which has not gone away. In Germany nowadays, they are calling themselves NSDAP. What's funny is that they still have a voice in the German parliament.

Besides, The NSDAP party is still functioning in the German parliament today; they operate worldwide under many other extremist groups. The idea of National Socialism, in my opinion, has not really gone away; it still with us, and it's going to be here for a very long time to come. If times get tough, people will turn from one extreme to another, whether it's extreme nationalism or communism. When that tough times come, they will have a very well-cultivated public. And the people in these tough times will be, unfortunately, more receptive to the message, whether of extreme nationalism or communism for that matter.

A SYMBOL OF THE SWASTIKA

INDIAN & TIBETAN BUDDHISM

THE BUDDIST TEMPLE IN INDIA

THE SYMBOL OF THE SUN

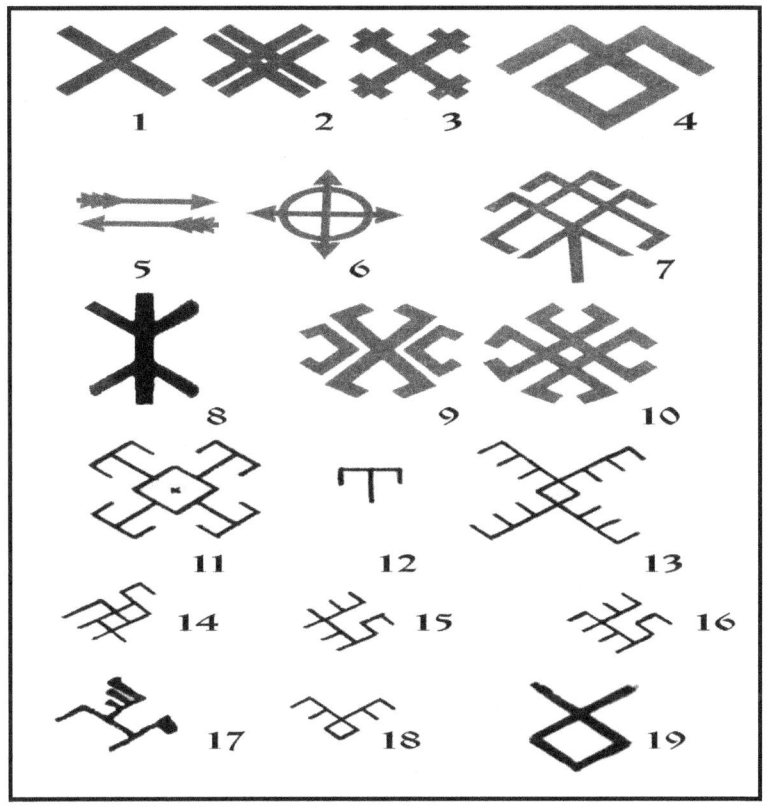

SLAVIC NUMERIC SYSTEM

CHAPTER 4

The Origins of the German/Nazi Swastika

We all been taught by our history teachers in our public schools that the German Nazi and Adolf Hitler adopted the symbol of the Swastika for their Nazi Party emblem. Later, they put the Swastika on the German flag between 1930 to 1945. However, that is all true; did you ever wonder from where the symbol of Swastika came? And was it always been lumped together with evil? As a historian, I will try to answer this question in this particular chapter.

The symbol of Swastika comes from Indian and Tibetan Buddhism. The Swastika symbolizes good fortune. However, in the 1930s, the Nazis or the National Socialists adopted it for their own purposes. The symbol Swastika is not only present in Tibetan and Indian Buddhism. It is also present in the Benedictine Christian Catholic order and adopted as their own symbol in the old days. The Swastika was even present in the ancient Slavic culture, as well and symbolized the sun. Even the holiday of Christmas, before it became the holiday, it was a pagan festival of Saturnalia. The day of the sun god, according to the Slavic legend, was born. So, Swastika in the ancient Slavic culture was just as important as the Christian cross is vital to Christianity. Maybe you didn't realize that Christianity arrived in Europe in the early 15th century. In this case, Intel the arrival of Christianity in Europe, most of Eastern Europe, and some other parts had so-called pagan beliefs. Sometimes they were called early Slavic beliefs, and yes, the so-called Swastika symbol has played a significant role in those ancient Slavic societies.

The other symbol that we will be discussing in this chapter is the

German SS Rune, were based on the ancient Slavic alphabet. The ancient Slavic Runes are still the oldest writing system from the ancient European continent. According to some sources, ancient Slavic society is just as old as ancient Islamic societies.

Who are the ancient Slavic people?

This is a very interesting question; the Slavic people are the people that live in Eastern Europe today. To some degree, the ancient Vikings might be included in that as well. Back in those ancient days, some of the Islamic traditions and Slavic traditions did blend. An excellent example of this would be their share of metallurgy and medicine, especially regarding trade and exchange of knowledge between cultures.

Did you know that the Slavic people had even kings of their own tribes in ancient times? So, as you can see, the German culture between the years 1920 to 1945 took many symbols and other markings exactly from an ancient, Slavic culture.

I know what you're thinking right about now; how come we are not being taught these things in our history classes in public schools? You have to understand that your education is controlled by the powers that be these particular powers. However, they do not want you to be educated, but they want you to be an obedient sheep that will be happy to March into the new globalist and one-world society. They do not let you think for yourself. However, all they want you to do is think their way. Education does not mean just sitting in a classroom and regurgitate what is written in your textbooks.

As our dear teachers like to put it, a truly educated and well-rounded person must understand history from all angles, whether bad, good, or ugly. Knowledge is the most powerful thing that a person can possess. You have to realize that one of the Roman emperors said that history is written by the victors. To some degree, he was right. However, if you want to be a truly educated individual, you have to learn every part of history. In fact, that is what this book will help you do. It will show you that your history sometimes is not what it seems, and your learning process should never stop.

KIMMEL ABDUL NASSER

HE WAS THE PRESIDENT OF EYGPT FROM 1970-1981.

MOHAMMED AMIN AL-MUSSEINI

HE WAS THE LEADER OF THE MUSLIMS FROM 1895 TO 1974

FLAG OF THE INDIAN UNIT

INDIAN WHITE TIGER UNIT

CHAPTER 5

The Black and the Arab Soldiers of the Third Reich

This is a very interesting part that is never talked about of World War II history. Did you know that Black and Arab soldiers also served in the German army between the years 1939 to 1945? Did you also know that many Indian soldiers also served in the German army during World War II? They all served under Field Marshal Erwin Rommel in Africa core. They also served in Italy, Normandy, France, and Greece. There were even some Arab/Black soldiers under the command of the move of Jerusalem; all mean all Husseini.

Your next question will be, who was Erwin Rommel?

Erwin Rommel was born, November 15, 1891, in Southern Germany. He did have a good understanding of desert warfare and its tactics. His mother's name was Helene Von Lutz; she did come from a privileged German family. He was part of the German government under the Austro-Hungarian German Empire, and yes, she might have been of Jewish descent; however, this is speculation.

His father served as an artillery officer in the German army during World War I. Thanks to his knowledge and understanding of the desert landscape, Erwin Rommel was posted to the Middle East, where he met most of Jerusalem Amin al-Husseini.

That is where the story of the Black soldiers of the Third Reich begins. Most of the Black soldiers were recruited from countries like Algeria, Ethiopia, Iraq, and Eritrea.

So, who was the Misty of Jerusalem between 1920 – 1945?

His full name was Mohammed Amin al-Husseini; he was the leader of the Muslims in Jerusalem from1895 Intel 1974. Some very big Indian units served in the German army between 1940 through 1945. Sometimes those units were referred to as the German Foreign Legion or the Indian White Tigers.

Those units were deployed to Normandy to boost up the German Atlantic wall. Those units also served with Amin al-Husseini, in the Balkans and former Yugoslavia through 1945.

Here is an interesting fact: some of the dreaded German SS policies came from two Indian religions. One of them is called Maha Barta, and the other one is called the Bono. When Geeta, the barn of a Geeta book itself, introduced the class system practiced in India to this day. Those two books did influence the policies of the German dreaded SS.

I know your following questions: how come when Jesse Owens won the gold medal in 1936 during the Olympic Games? Why didn't Adolf Hitler show up, give him, or present to him his gold medal? Was he a racist? To this particular question, I am never afraid of answering. He might not have shown up to present Jesse Owens his gold medal during the 1936 Olympics because he was ashamed that Germany lost the race. However, this is only speculation because we still live in a free country, and we can still question the history presented to us in our dear old public school, where they are training us. Still, they are not educating you because there is a difference between training and education. After all, an educated person can think and make up his mind about different things. However, a trained person has been trained just to regurgitate things that he was trying to say. However, a person like that does not have the capability to think for himself. That is the difference between me and my books. My books will teach you how to think for yourself and reason also hold an argument or a discussion.

One of the Black/Arab soldiers, who served in the German army, might have been the ex-president of Egypt, Kemal Abdul Nasser's name. He served as the president of Egypt from June 23, 1956 – September 28, 1970. The other soldier who might have served in the German army during World War II was Anwar Sadat. He was the third president of Egypt; he was in office between October 5, 1970, and October 6, 1981. For sure, those two presidents of Egypt were influenced by the Islamic leader, al-Husseini.

However, we have to ask ourselves the following question: Were these Arab leaders using the Germans back in the 1930s and 40s to pursue their own nation's political and nationalistic agendas?

What you have to understand is that when it comes to deep study of World War II, everyone used everyone else to accomplish their own political ambitions/goals. This is nothing new; it happens in today's politics as well. In this case, I think those African leaders also used their own people for their own political or nationalistic agendas. We can especially see it when India tried to achieve its own independence goals from Great Britain, when they joined the German army, and World War II in some Indian regions.

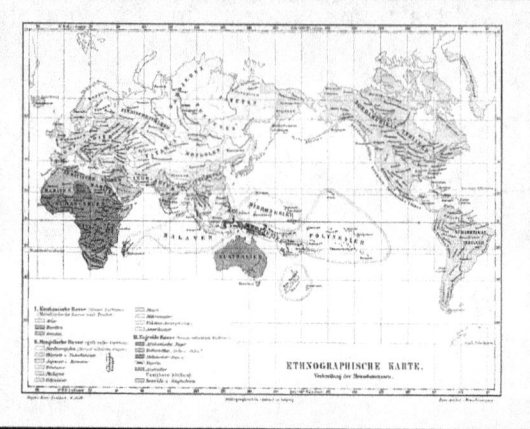

WHERE ARYAN PEOPLE CAME FROM

WHAT THE ARYAN PEOPLE MAY LOOK LIKE

Mohenjo Daro

THE ANCIENT ARYANS HAVE CONDUCTED THEIR NUCLEAR EXPERIMENTS WITH NUCLEAR TECHNOLOGY

CHAPTER 6

Was the Aryan Race Real or Fake

After careful research, I have to say that the Aryan people were real. Some of them are still living on this earth today, and countries like India, Pakistan, Afghanistan, and Iran. So, the Aryan race was not blonde-haired and blue-eyed people. In this case, you are correct; they were not White, blonde with blue eyes. Those people and their ancestors today are mostly of Indian or Iranian or even Afghan descent.

The myth of blue-eyed and blonde hair Aryan was built up by the Nazi Party during World War II to pursue their sick agenda. They were not from the city of Atlantis like some of the legends said. There are speculations and strong evidence that the real Aryan did possess some advanced knowledge of nuclear technology.

Their most advanced city was the city of Mohan Joe Dara on the India-Pakistan border. This is where the ancient Aryans have conducted their nuclear experiments with nuclear technology.

How can we be sure that this is true?

It is true because the radiation levels in Mohan Joe Dara's city are still unacceptable for human beings, and no one lives there to this very day. The ancient Aryan race also had a very advanced knowledge of metallurgy.

Your next question should be, do you believe in ancient astronaut theory?

In this case, this book is not about ancient astronaut theory. However, this book is about, secrets of World War II. We have to acknowledge that

Aryans' ancient race did possess secret technology that has helped them discover how to work with metals and maybe have possessed secret technology and advanced knowledge of things like mathematics, geometry, chemistry, and some other things.

I know what you are thinking; what about Charles Darwin's theory that a man and other humans have evolved from apes? May I say as a scientist Charles Darwin has the right to propose his own theory of evolution? But we still have to acknowledge that there were very advanced human beings, even before Charles Darwin and his creation eight theory. We have to understand that ancient Aryans who lived in Iran, Pakistan, and India possessed the knowledge of the written word. The Aryan race reached the country known today as Afghanistan. In this case, the Aryans who lived, of course, possessed a very advanced written language thousands of years ago and may be more advanced technology than we have today.

We can definitely say that in the city of manager Doro, in Pakistan the Aryans in ancient time, they did have a nuclear power plant to power up its vast electrical and computer network, they could even produce what we call artificial gold, that's right ladies and gentlemen the ancient Aryans, not aliens, had the power to produce artificial gold which is then they could use to produce and maintain their own computer and electronic equipment, although this is only speculation.

When it comes to the city of Mohan Joe Dara and the ancient Aryan race, their civilization must have collapsed due to an accident in their own ancient nuclear power plant; this is only a theory.

You have to realize that sometimes the history books do not tell you the whole story about certain subjects. And that is okay because, in reality, all textbooks, especially history textbooks, can only take you so far on your journey. But the rest of the way, you will have to take the journey further by yourself.

You will have to use other resources to get information. As far as we can see, the ancient Aryans themselves are not even mentioned in the mainstream history books. Still, there are other resources out there, such as the Internet, to further your knowledge about this particular subject and many others. This is, by the way, a very good thing, in my opinion.

The ancient Aryans might have even had the knowledge of flight because, just like the Egyptians, they were constructing flight machines, like your average glider airplane today. The hardest thing about learning about the subject of ancient Aryans, not ancient aliens, mind you is that the information is asked. However, even with the use of the Internet, it is hard to get information about this particular subject. The ancient Aryans themselves are even more technically advanced than we are right now. But because they were so dependent on their so-called marble of technology, that they got careless with it. Yes, I am very much for the advance of technology in the world. The only thing is that we cannot get careless with it as the ancient Aryans did. So, in this case, for you to get more knowledge about the ancient Aryan people in real life, you have to go beyond your regular history grade school or high school textbook.

You also have to realize that your education, whether in high school or in universities, is controlled. Therefore, when it comes to your history knowledge that is also being controlled by the powers, that be.

One wise man said that knowledge is power and I think, in this case, he was right. Nowadays, things are even getting better because, in reality, for you to seek the knowledge, you don't have to look for it far and wide.

However, I will also tell you that sometimes such knowledge about ancient Aryans that we are discussing in this particular chapter can sometimes be misused by the people who apply it for their own purposes.

There are some people in this world that, in the upcoming decade, will try to stop us from seeking this particular knowledge about the ancient Aryans, for example.

How are they going to accomplish this?

In their eyes, if you are not qualified or you don't have that degree in history, for example. Then, in that case, when you present the knowledge about ancient Aryans, then you will be laughed at and made fun of by the scientific and academic so-called community. You have to understand that this knowledge is relatively new when you present this type of knowledge that I am giving in this particular chapter. So, in that case, sometimes people will not know how to respond to this particular knowledge. Sometimes, the scientific community and the people who control our education system will not let you share this specific knowledge with the rest of the world because all it comes down to is money and a monopoly on education.

Although the ancient Aryans were a very advanced race of human beings, there is practically no room for them in our controlled so-called history books. Because certain people in our world love to have control and monopoly on the basic knowledge that we consume in our schools and universities.

The ancient Aryans might have spoken the language of ancient

Aramaic, the language of Aramaic. Aramaic is the grandfather of the Arabic language itself. The other language that ancient Aryan ancestors might have been speaking is the language of the Pashto language. It is said today in some parts of Afghanistan and Pakistan. The other language that the ancient Aryans might have used was called Farsi, or a dialect of it.

What is Farsi, you may ask?

Farsi is the Persian language that is spoken in Iran today. It is a version of the Arabic language, but not entirely.

So, as you can see, the Aryans were part of a very advanced civilization.

However, when we look at our textbooks today, some say that man has evolved from an ape. That is the theory of creation by Mr. Charles Darwin. In this case, I would disagree with this particular theory because how can a people with such advanced knowledge of metallurgy gold making and other valuable skills have evil from an ape? Yes, Aryan people did exist in the world; however, they were not blonde and blue-eyed people. They are more related to the Arab people and the Indian people of today. Some of them went as far as Pakistan, Afghanistan, and Iran. My question to you is, how come we are always taught when it comes to this theory of creation that a person involved from an ape? When we have evidence that some civilizations have had such advanced technology like the Aryans or the Indians, or even the ancient. All I'm saying is that Charles Darwin's theory of creation or evolution; I think it needs to be reevaluated because this theory may have some flaws in it.

THE ACTUAL TIME MACHINE

THE ACTUAL WRECKAGE IN KECKSBURG, PENNSYLVANIA

THIS PICTURE SHOWS WHERE THE ACTUAL TESTING TOOK PLACE IN POLAND

CHAPTER 7

The German Time Machine

Did, you know that during World War II, the Germans researched the possibility of time travel?

Yes, they researched in the area of time travel, but not only that, there is evidence that they did have a working prototype that worked and was able to transport people back and forth through time. This was called the D Glock, an experiment or the bell that was developed in Poland. During World War II, the Germans and the Nazis conducted those experiments on time travel. And what's even fascinating about that is that they did have a working prototype.

Although some people try to discredit the theories of the author of the paper or book, Mr. Igor V, and we can definitely prove that the bell or the prototype of the Time Machine worked. We have to look at what happened during the so-called Kecksburg incident in Pennsylvania in the United States in December 1965. In this case, with the evidence presented, we would have to say that yes, the Time Machine worked. Although the Kecksburg Pennsylvania is referred to as a UFO incident. We can safely say that this was not a UFO incident. However, we can call a Time Machine experiment that worked from the documents available on the subject.

The second part of this particular discussion is that those people like Dr. Hans Kammler and many others traveled through time in 1965 during the Kicks Berg Pennsylvania incident? The second question must have been, did the Americans bring the Time Machine parts and made it work in their secret laboratory in area 51? Some say that Dr. Hans Kammler was responsible for the work, and the Time Machine experiments in Poland disappeared. That is because nobody can tell what's happened to the people like Dr. Hans Kammler and many others who have led worked on this particular project of time travel.

The other person who thought that time travel was even possible was Albert Einstein himself, by proposing the theory of relativity and other mathematical and practical things that made time travel possible.

Maybe such people like Dr. Hans Kammler and his coworkers and scientists who worked on the D Glock project/Time Machine project came to the United States and continued their work in places like area 51 or one of many secret military installations in the United States. In this case, we can safely say that the actual Time Machine may exist here in the US from the evidence I have gathered.

I know that this is only speculation; however, the bigger question is, what if this is the actual truth that time travel is not only a so-called dream but what if that time travel is a reality due to the ability of reverse in you nearing? So, in this case, the reality of time travel might be true.

We have to remember that Dr. Hans Kammler was not the only one working on the D Glock/Time Machine project. The other people who worked on this Time Machine project of the Glock are Maria Orsic, Dr. Hans Kammler, Alfred Rosenberg, Heinrich Himmler, and Dr. Theodor Morell. Those people were part of the technical class or technicians, which were part of the Vereal Society, and some were part of the Thule Society. In reality, nobody knows what happened to Alford Rosenberg. He was, after all, a founder of the Vereal Society. There is speculation that the Nazi Party had eliminated Alfred Rosenberg after he was no longer of use to them. However, there is stronger speculation that Alford Rosenberg has escaped with the Time Machine with people like Hans Kammler and other members of the Vereal Society and the Thule Society.

Such scientists as Dr. Von Braun and many others, who were bought to the United States by the US government\ to help us in our rocket program, were possibly members of the Thule Society and the Vereal society.

CHAPTER 8

The Holocaust Industry

This chapter will cover a very controversial topic that is most prevalent today: the issue of the Holocaust Industry that is practiced by the Jewish community today.

What is the Holocaust Industry?

The Holocaust Industry is a practice that the Jewish community uses worldwide to get more money from people worldwide for their tiny state of Israel. What is more disgusting about this is that those people have no respect for their own dead relatives. That is because they are making billions of dollars, and they are profiting from their relative's deaths in the concentration camps of World War II. Let me clarify the experience of World War II, and the concentration camps were a big tragedy for the Jewish people and the entire world. However, the sickest part of this entire endeavor is how to Jewish people and the state of Israel is exploiting the tragedy of the Holocaust.

Here is how the whole scam works, and here are some ways that people worldwide are being scammed. Let me give you an example of Rob I. Eckstein and his stupid idea of the fellowship of Christians and Jews. On American TV, what Rob I. Eckstein does, is running a commercial where he shows the so-called poor people in Israel and how bad the living conditions are. You have to remember that those commercials on TV are designed to play on American people's emotions. And in those commercials when he bags the American people to give money to support Israel. He plays on the emotional card by using Auschwitz's tragedy to help the American people part with their money.

The other person who illustrates this issue a little bit deeper is Dr. Norm Finkelstein, Benny's book The Holocaust Industry. Let's, at this point, make something clear and understood. During World War II, not only the Jewish people suffered in the concentration camp, but there were such nationalities as the Polish people, the Gypsies, and many other nations that suffered as well. The media does not mention this particular fact, or if they do, they mention it and such a passive way.

Let us take a look at who killed the Jewish people during World War II in reality. Names such as Reinhard Heidrick, Adolf Eichmann, and many others who came from a prominent Jewish family. Even Adolf Hitler himself was Jewish because his real name is Adolf Sickle Gruber before his father changed it to Hitler, as I mentioned at the beginning of this book.

However, the bigger question you have to ask yourself is why they executed Adolf Eichmann so fast? Is it that Adolf Eichmann was Jewish, or he had some Jewish roots? And the Jews didn't want the people to find that out? If people knew this, it would be difficult for the Jews to make such a tragedy.

Look, I know that some people may call me all kinds of names after reading this book. Nonetheless, I'm addressing this issue to the American taxpayer. I really don't care one way or the other whether you support Israel or not. Just know that as an American taxpayer, you are being used, that's all. You see, in reality, I'm a capitalist too; however, I would never exploit such a tragedy, like the Holocaust, to make money. In my opinion, exploiting such a tragedy is more than disgusting. And what's even more sickening is how the Jews in America are playing on people's emotions and using Auschwitz's tragedy to get rich. How low can you go to make money? An Arab prostitute has more class than the Jews in this case.

After careful research, I concluded that World War II was fought between two ideologies. One of them, was the Jewish left, that was presented by the Judeo Bolsheviks/communist and the Jewish right that was, presented by the Nationalist Socialist Party of Germany. Let us look at the issue, from a different perspective, if there were 150,000 soldiers of Jewish descent in the German army between 1939 and 1945, and who knows, how many of them joined the dreaded German SS.

There is a very interesting history about Adolf Eichmann, and that is that he was fascinated by the Jewish culture, and he did speak Hebrew. What's even funnier, most of his relatives were Jewish also. So, what are we to conclude from all this was adult Eichmann the most notorious member of the German SS, Jewish by birth?

That is a very interesting question; however, we will not find the right answers. But, after careful research, we would have to come to our own conclusions. The speculation is after careful research by many, historians that have dealt with this issue extensively came to the closing conclusion that, in reality, he actually might have been Jewish. In this case, that is why Israel wanted to get rid of him quickly so that no one would have found out that he was Jewish.

Therefore, fascism and Zionism are almost the same ideologies, but in different packages, that's all. This is my opinion, of course.

There are a lot of questions about World War II that have not been answered yet. What if there is evidence that Adolf Hitler or Adolf sickle Gruber did not die in that bunker in Berlin in 1945. We will try to examine this issue in the next chapter.

There are many questions about World War II that have not been answered yet. I realize that some of my research and questions about this particular subject are controversial. However, if the mainstream historians will not touch on such subjects as World War II and only give us bits and pieces of information, in that case, this is not cool. If he wants to study a subject, a truly educated person should study all of its aspects and not only the things that the educational, industrial complex will allow him to study. You have to understand that, yes, your education system is controlled by the powers that be. However, sometimes your education has to go beyond your regular school textbooks. Now I realize that sometimes learning about our history is not always pleasant. However, if we are permitted to call ourselves educated people, we must understand the subjects' good, bad, and ugly sides. You will not experience this in your regular educational system.

Some people may say that knowledge is power, and that is correct. However, if you want to obtain enlightenment and knowledge truly, you will have to go to other sources for that knowledge, even beyond your school materials.

HANA REITSCH IS THE PERSON WHO MIGHT HAVE BEEN DIRECTLY RESPONSIBLE FOR ADOLF HITLER'S ESCAPE

ARTHUR SKORZENY, AFTER WORLD WAR II, STARTED HIS OWN PRIVATE MILITARY COMPANY CALLED THE POLIDENT GROUP

CHAPTER 9

The Escape of Adolf Hitler

We all heard the story that Adolf Hitler has committed suicide in his bunker, under the chancellery at the end of the war on April 30, 1945. However, what if there is more to this story, than we are being told, and we were taught by our dear old teachers in our public schools. There is a possibility that Adolf Hitler has escaped Berlin during the last months of the war. And he escaped to the country of Argentina in South America.

We are all familiar with the Vatican Ratlines and how the Catholic Church was involved in helping the ex-Nazis escape to countries in South America, like Brazil and Argentina. However, you have to remember that there were many other places in the world where the ex-Nazi have escaped. Now we all know who has said that Adolf Hitler/Adolf sickle Gruber has killed himself in the bunker. However, the people who are behind the stories are the Russians.

We all know that the Russians said they had found two burnt bodies of Adolf Hitler and his mistress. Ava Brown burnt in the German chancellery building in 1945. However, they said that they could not make a positive ID in this case.

There is one gentleman who has studied this case thoroughly; his name is Bob Baer.

Who is Bob Baer, you might be asking?

Bob Baer, or Robert Baer, was a CIA agent during the Clinton administration and the Bush administration. He has experience in Lebanon and the Middle East; however, his famous or most famous work was on a case of possibilities of Adolf Hitler's escape during World War II.

We all know that Argentina's country was friendly to the ex-German Nazis in the late 40s throughout the early 50s to 1960.

At that time, Argentina was ruled by a dictator named Juan Perrone. At that time, President Juan Perrone of Argentina was sympathetic to the ex-fascist/Nazi. The possibility of Hitler's escape with the Vatican Ratline's help was and still is a very strong possibility.

Many people may have been responsible for the help of Adolf Hitler's escape at the end of World War II. However, the person who might have been directly responsible for Adolf Hitler's escape was a woman named Hana Reitsch.

Who was on the right, you might be asking?

Hana Reitsch was the first German woman aviator. She did fly some of the German World War II experimental aircraft. There is a possibility that she might have flown the first German helicopter.

So how does Hana Reitsch fit into Hitler's escape scenario?

Well, we all know that during the last days of World War II in Berlin, there was a lot of confusion, and things were chaotic. So, in that case, someone like Hana Reitsch could have pulled off with her airplane pilot expertise, such a piece of extraordinary flying. Let's remember that Hitler did not escape to Argentina by airplane. Nevertheless, an airplane might have been used to fly him out of Berlin and his family to a German submarine base where he could have taken a U-boat with his family to Argentina. Hana wrote herself and learned to fly on gliders in Zielona Gura, which is part of Poland. Her father was a local uptime mistress, so she did come from a prominent, well-to-do family; as you can see, she did.

You see, even the Russians at the end of World War II could not conclude whether the head that was found in the German chancellery in 1945, whether this was Adolf Hitler's skull or someone else. According to Bob Baer and his investigation, two people witnessed a German submarine's surfacing in 1945, right after World War II. As a matter of fact, there were two German submarines that surfaced in 1945 at that particular time.

Did Adolf Hitler really escape to Argentina? The evidence is very strong to entertain that possibility.

We all know that there were a lot of ex-Nazi/Germans that settled in Argentina. We also know that many ex-German officers also escaped to Middle Eastern countries like Egypt and many others. One of the ex-SS officers who have done this was Arthur scores any, which in this case he was what we call the German version of James Bond, so the possibility of the escape of a lot of ex-Nazi and German officers is a fact.

We also know that the Americans also conducted what we call Operation Paperclip. In which case, many German engineers who have built the V1 and V2 rockets came to the United States and worked on the American space program. One of the people who did that was the famous Dr. Von Braun and many other German scientists did that.

We also know that the American Central intelligence agency, the CIA for short, had also employed ex-German/Nazi officers when we were fighting the Cold War against the Soviets as well.

There is a possibility that the CIA employed a German gentleman by the name of Clouse Bart during the Cold War against the Soviets. Many of the CIA tactics used against the Soviet Union during the Cold War were actually taught to our CIA operatives by those ex-SS/German officers.

As far as Arthur Skorzeny after World War II, he started his own private military company called the Polident Group. However, this particular company did not do any private security work, like your private military contractors do today overseas. However, this particular company did export what we call terrorism to the Middle East. This particular company was teaching the Arabs guerrilla warfare tactics. As far as we know, and we can certainly speculate, Arthur Skorzeny is the person who rescued Benito Mussolini in Italy and World War II is spent most of his life in Egypt. Where did he and his family find a safe haven? Arthur Skorzeny and the Central Intelligence Agency sponsored the Polident Group, the CIA, to train the Egyptian military.

He also taught and actually helped form other countries, special operations forces, and the intelligence services as well.

We will now discuss the Catholic Church's involvement in helping the ex-Nazi escape to the west and other countries after World War II.

The Vatican, to facilitate this particular endeavor, has set up the Ratlines. They worked like the American Underground Railroad. After World War II, the Vatican has provided the money and other means for the ex-Nazis to escape justice and start their lives all over again in countries like Spain, Argentina, and many other places as well. Some of them have even escaped to the Middle East and adopted their new Muslim identity as well. Rumor has it that Arthur Skorzeny has helped set up the Israeli Intelligence Liquidation Squads. For a time, he did work for the Israeli Intelligence Networks as a private military contractor. He ended up living in Spain after his contract and the Middle East has ended. However, he played both sides against each other in the Middle East.

In the next chapter, we will be discussing a very interesting secret of World War II and the involvement of the Catholic Church in the escape of the ex-Nazi after World War II out of Germany.

There is still a large German community in the Middle East, South America, and countries like Brazil, Bolivia, etc. There is also a large German community and countries like Egypt, Lebanon, and many other places in the Middle East. Rumor also has it that the dreaded Dr. Amendola also escaped from Germany in 1945. And he has spent the rest of his life in Brazil as well. Dr. Mangalore did come from a prominent, influential family as well.

So, as you can see, most of those people did come from wealth. So, in that case, whether they were Jewish or not, it did not matter. That is because they could buy their way out of that predicament. Being wealthy just as today does have its privileges, just like it was true back in the late 20s and early 30s.

CHAPTER 10

The Vatican and the Third Reich

In this particular chapter, we will be discussing another unknown secret of World War II and that is the involvement of the Vatican with the Third Reich after World War II and may be even during World War II itself.

Some of you may not know that the Catholic Church in the Vatican itself has its own bank.

Yes, some people may say that the Vatican bank does not exist. However, the institution of Vatican Bank does exist, although the Catholic Church itself may be denying it. During World War II, the Vatican may have some financial dealings with the Nazis and the Third Reich.

I guess by now, you all heard of the so-called Hitler Pope; his name was Pope Pius XII, sometimes he was referred to as the Hitler's Pope.

After World War II, the Catholic Church, the Vatican, and the Vatican bank started up what we call the Ratlines. The Ratlines worked like the Underground Railroad, which helped the German ex-Nazi escape to places like the Middle East or South America. The Vatican provided the ex-Nazi with money and passports so that they could start their new lives in South America or the Middle East. That is because, in the Vatican itself, there were a lot of bishops who were pro-German/Nazi ideology. One of them was Clemens August Graf von Galen. He was part of the Vatican in 1946. Also, the Ratlines themselves were possibly founded or funded by the Vatican Bank. The Vatican has also provided those ex-Nazis with Red Cross passports. The Vatican also provided them with different identities so that the ex-Nazis could live the rest of their lives in different countries.

We all know that the Catholic Vatican was involved in collaboration with the fascist government during World War II.

The next question, we should ask ourselves what other shenanigans and corruption is the Vatican involved in now are they supporting Isis?

Or any other national right-wing or left-wing group or groups, for that matter?

We will never know the answers to these questions; however, we do have the right to ask them as educated people. We also, as educated people, not trained people, can definitely speculate and make a hypothesis about different things. We have to admit the Vatican has done many negative things like corruption and the destruction of the Knights Templar order. The Vatican destroyed the Knights Templar because of their knowledge about different things.

Nowadays, there is speculation that the Vatican Bank has laundered money for the Mafia and who knows what else and who else. The Vatican might have even committed some crimes because they liquidated the chief banking official from the Vatican Bank name Bartel Calvi. He was the chief banking officer at the Vatican Bank. There are rumors that after World War II, the Vatican Bank and the intelligence agencies have worked together during the Cold War up to now. The Vatican also made deals with the Rothschild banking Empire during and after World War II.

We will not truly know the extent of the corruption that is going on in the Vatican to this day. That is because the Vatican is basically its own sovereign country. In reality, we don't know what is going on in the Vatican today, especially what kind of knowledge and does the Vatican possess within their Vatican secret archive. That is why it is important to have a very informed public because, as we all know by now, knowledge is power and no one can take that away from you. Knowledge is especially important now because the decisions that affect all of our lives are not made in our capitals anymore. However, they are made by what we call world government and this is where we must be very careful. We have to be fairly knowledgeable about different issues.

The Vatican is not only guilty of child abuse in the United States. However, this disgusting thing did not only happen here; it happened in Canada as well. It happened in Québec during the late 40s and early 50s. This type of scandal also happened in the country of Ireland. I guess you heard of the Magdalene Laundries. This is where the Catholic Church has claimed to put single mothers, prostitutes, and other undesirable women to make them into slaves, work them, and tell them they could not work anymore. There are speculations that the Catholic Church has turned those women into "Ladies of the Night," if you get the meaning.

So, as you can see, the Vatican itself did collaborate with the Nazis during World War II. However, the Vatican itself is also guilty of other things as well.

The Vatican itself is using the Christian religion to collect money and basically to control the people. Let's face it, the connection between the Rothschild banking Empire and the Vatican itself is very clear, and as we know, the Rothschilds banking Empire and the Vatican are part of what we call the Globalists One-World Government.

So, in this case, we can say with certainty that the Catholic religion and the globalists who could, or who tried to control the world work together hand-in-hand to control the world and its population through religion, so that the people can be led to the so-called globalist government without question, like a bunch of sheep all.

Let's face it if the Rothschild banking Empire and the five Vatican get-together, we all know that something is wrong with this picture, we cannot say for sure what that is, but something is not right in this case.

CHAPTER 11

Control of the Population Through Religion

Control of the population through religion, although it is a controversial subject, we can certainly examine it in this book.

If the deals were made between the Vatican between the Rothschild Banking Empire and the Vatican, we could safely say that controlling the population through religion is possible.

We all know that such people like the Rothschild banking Empire the Morgan's and the Rockefellers and many others are in favor of. Let's call this one-world government, and I would bet that those people will definitely use any means necessary to accomplish their goals, including using the Catholic Church and the deals they make between themselves, to accomplish their goals of one-world government.

My question is if in the Jewish Bible it says that when the Jews escape from Egypt, they were marching through the desert for 40 years, okay it also says that God gave them manna from heaven to eat, my question is so when the Jews were being marched to the concentration camps during World War II how come God did not give them manna to eat or help them to escape in that case, so in this case, those stories I would think that yes those stories in the Judeo Christian Bible are basically designed to control the population and what is hidden behind all of this is large sums of money. The Christian church and the Catholic Church, in this case, basically have money, has power, and it has control of the so-called sheep, all not people but sheep all.

Look, I really don't care, by what name you call your God, whether you are religious or not, that is no business of mine. However, what I'm trying to do in my books is give you a look at the world from a different perspective. And as educated people that we can call ourselves, we have to seek knowledge and question everything that is happening around us, especially regarding history, science, and other subjects. When you even question science, that's okay too. That is because that's how discoveries are made in the scientific community by actually questioning the status quo.

Some people in the European countries can say if you do not have an education in history, you have nothing to say about a certain subject like history. For example, however, this is wrong because let's face it, discoveries can come from different directions. If you are interested in certain subjects, you should be able to do your own research freely, and you should also be able to share your research with the marketplace. Let's put it this way the Catholic Church and the established academic and historical institutions do not have monopolies on historical knowledge that we can share, and we can certainly discover.

Questions and discoveries are not only meant to be discovered by the academic religious or any other established monopoly in this universe. Suppose we are interested in certain subjects and have sufficient knowledge of those particular subjects. In that case, I think we all have some things to consider and add to the scientific, historical, and any other academic subjects in the academic or research world. If we want to be knowledgeable and educated people, we should not worry about what other people will think of us.

The story of the Manna from Heaven, in the Bible it may be true; however, this manna itself was made by a machine, that the Israelites have taken it from Egypt, and there was no such thing as the ark of the cabinet what was the ark itself it was. This atomic reactor powered the manna machine.

So, in this case, yes, the Rothschilds and the Vatican and other Christian mainstream religions are leading us into one-world government because those people think that they have a monopoly on such a thing as speculation and knowledge. Unfortunately, they are very wrong in this case.

In an open and educated society, if someone has something interesting to contribute to the research of any type of scientific literature or any other academic discipline, then they should be allowed to do so without any restrictions or bashing from the academic community.

The academic community can be a friend to a person who does his own research on certain subjects. However, some in the academic community think that certain research is presented because I have a degree in whatever scientific or academic field. After all, they have a degree, which means that they know everything about a given subject.

That is not true because things like science and any other subjects do evolve and change so, the academic establishment does not have a monopoly or not. Neither does the Christian and Catholic establishment have a monopoly on knowledge.

If we want to survive and thrive in the so-called New World Order, then it is up to us to educate ourselves and continue seeking knowledge and wisdom in whatever subject we choose. We cannot allow other people to dictate what you want to study or how you want to seek knowledge to be the best-informed citizen.

This is how in some cases, you can defeat the so-called Global Governance/New World Order and the internationalist who want to turn us into the sheep all.

The best thing to defeat the globalists and their new world agenda is actually knowledge and very well-informed public, that means when we study something whether it's history or anything else we should study every aspect of it, not only what is written in our public school's textbooks if you really want to seek knowledge then you should go beyond your regular school textbooks because there is knowledge beyond such things like textbooks. In this case, knowledge is power, so if we want to be a very informed public, it is up to us to seek it. Your real education and true education begin when you leave your so-called educational establishment behind. Then you truly can do your research and form your own opinions. And test whether what you are thinking about was correct or not. That is because, in today's so-called educational establishment, they can only teach you how to think their way. There is no outside-of-the-box thinking in today's educational establishment. When you want to seek knowledge on your own you will have to go outside of your comfort zone and outside of your educational establishment and monopolize those types of institutions.

1. Is it okay to question what you are being taught in a so-called educational establishment?

The answer to that particular question is an absolute yes.

2. Is the educational establishment always correct in what they're teaching you? It all depends.

This is because the educational establishment does not give you true education.

So yes, your real education can truly begin once you get out of the so-called educational establishment because then and only then will you be able to make up your own mind about certain things in this world.

ABOUT THE AUTHOR

Mark Wrobel resides in Wilmington, Delaware, and was born with a disability. But it didn't allow that to stop him from excelling in life. His father raised Mark; he was a dedicated single parent. He grew up in a communist system. Due to his disability, his country would not allow him to attend school with regular kids, but he persevered. Fortunately, when he was about 10 years old, he came to the United States, which he knew was the land of opportunity. So, he took full advantage of it and made sure he got a good education.

From 1989 until 1993, he attended St. Thomas The Apostle School, a Catholic school in Wilmington, Delaware.

Then in 1993, he attended Wilmington High School and graduated in 1997 with a high school diploma.

In 2002, Mark attended Delaware Tech Community College to attend their Web Designer Certificate Program, which he completed.

He continued his education in 2008 at Strayer University, studying Information Systems and Homeland Security. Mark graduated from Stayer in 2012 with an Associate Degree.

In 2018, he returned to Strayer University to obtain his Bachelor of

Science Degree in Information Systems and Homeland Security Management and graduated in 2020. He is proud of this accomplishment because he was told that it was impossible and he couldn't do it.

Mark is currently employed with the United States Coast Guards in Communications. He began working for the Coast Guard in 2012. Thus far, he has received multiple awards and accolades for his dedicated service. Mark loves to learn and try new things.

In 2007, he decided to try sky diving and with the help of an instructor, he jumped 18,000 feet. There was an article published about it in the News Journal.

In the future, he would like to go back to school to obtain his master's and a doctoral degree.

Mark is the author of the titles Start of the Coming Civil War, Progressive Credentialism Versus Ageism, and The American Holocaust, which are available online worldwide. Unknown Secrets of World War II is his fourth book, and he couldn't have done it without his father's support.

REFERENCES

Hitler's Jewish Soldiers

https://www.youtube.com/watch?v=-Fh7hQScY4M

https://www.youtube.com/watch?v=kjGJhcsw20U

https://www.youtube.com/watch?v=ddvpMvzVX24

https://bryanmarkrigg.com/

https://spartacus-educational.com/GERmiltch.htm

https://www.historyplace.com/worldwar2/biographies/heydrich-biography.htm

https://www.jta.org/1961/04/21/archive/eichmann-claims-he-had-many-jewish-relatives-says-he-is-no-

https://en.wikipedia.org/wiki/Josef_Mengele#Early_life

https://spartacus-educational.com/GERhitler.htm

https://en.wikipedia.org/wiki/Erich_von_Manstein

https://en.wikipedia.org/wiki/Alois_Hitler

https://www.youtube.com/watch?v=cm1xLCOLVkY

Origins of the Swastika

https://www.lotussculpture.com/blog/meaning-swastika-buddhism-hinduism/

https://reclaimingzen.com/the-buddhist-swastika/

https://www.catholicculture.org/culture/library/dictionary/index.cfm?id=36738

The Real Aryans

https://www.ancient-origins.net/history-famous-people/true-aryans-who-were-they-really-and-how-were-their-origins-corrupted-009075

https://en.wikipedia.org/wiki/Aryan_race

https://www.youtube.com/watch?v=7zx1xx4Tqh0

https://www.britannica.com/topic/Aramaic-language

https://www.britannica.com/place/Mohenjo-daro

Black Soldiers in the German Army, 1939 to 1945

https://archive.org/details/hitlers-arab-black-soldiers-one-of-the-strangest-units-in-the-german-army-during

https://www.youtube.com/watch?v=QTaEuaVIFtQ

Indian Soldiers in the German Army Between 1939 – 1945

https://www.feldgrau.com/WW2-German-Wehrmacht-Indian-Volunteers/

https://en.wikipedia.org/wiki/Indian_Legion

How Did the Nora Berg laws Actually Work

https://www.youtube.com/watch?v=-Fh7hQScY4M

Dr. Hans Kammler

https://military.wikia.org/wiki/Hans_Kammler

Dr. von Braun

https://en.wikipedia.org/wiki/Wernher_von_Braun

Organizations Who Put the Nazi party in Power

https://en.wikipedia.org/wiki/Vril

https://www.altereddimensions.net/2012/the-vril-society

https://en.wikipedia.org/wiki/Thule_Society

https://exopolitics.org/german-secret-societies-hid-ancient-super-weapons-from-nazis/

https://en.wikipedia.org/wiki/Rudolf_von_Sebottendorf

https://scarenormal.com/the-secret-vril-society/

https://en.wikipedia.org/wiki/Alfred_Rosenberg

https://en.wikipedia.org/wiki/Illuminati

The Other Origins of the Nazi Symbols

https://www.messagetoeagle.com/oldest-writing-system-among-slavs-to-be-germanic-runes-new-study/

https://womeninahomeoffice.com/know-yourself/slavic-runes-and-their-meaning.html

https://slaviablog.wordpress.com/2014/06/08/slavic-vikings/

https://survincity.com/2012/12/runes-of-ancient-slavs/

The Nazi Party Today in Germany

http://www.nsdap.info/

The Vatican Bank

https://vatican.com/The-Vatican-Bank/

Vatican and the Third Reich

https://en.wikipedia.org/wiki/Pope_Pius_XII

https://www.youtube.com/watch?v=LyfS5N8g6-Y

https://www.cbc.ca/news/canada/montreal/duplessis-orphans-meet-irish-mother-baby-homes-1.4142930

https://en.wikipedia.org/wiki/Otto_Skorzeny#:~:text=Otto%20Skorzeny%20%28left%29%20and%20Juan%20Per%C3%B3n%20%28center%29.%20In,the%20CIA%29%20to%20act%20as%20Naguib%27s%20military%20advisor.

https://elementamundi.com/otto-skorzeny-and-the-paladin-group/

https://www.historyandheadlines.com/vatican-city-orgy-50-prostitutes-entertain-papal-palace/

https://www.youtube.com/watch?v=tqN_Q3QNhJY

Nazi Working for the Israeli Intelligence

https://www.youtube.com/watch?v=tqN_Q3QNhJY now

Escape of Adolf Hitler

https://en.wikipedia.org/wiki/Hanna_Reitsch

https://en.wikipedia.org/wiki/Juan_Per%C3%B3n

https://www.youtube.com/watch?v=bXmo9sCMjIM

https://www.youtube.com/watch?v=mX5aSLYzdgI

Here is How the American People are Being Used

https://www.amazon.com/Holocaust-Industry-Reflections-Exploitation-Suffering/dp/1781685614

https://www.youtube.com/watch?v=yN9QWERUAf4

Two Most Influential Books that Influenced the Third Reich

https://www.amazon.com/Bhagavad-Gita-2nd-Eknath-Easwaran/dp/1586380192?ref_=Oct_s9_apbd_obs_hd_bw_b3Fk&pf_rd_r=XQGT2VDZM2QKTNP9PKNJ&pf_rd_p=b7a9379a-2b86-5d3f-870b-0f4be7aa32fc&pf_rd_s=merchandised-search-10&pf_rd_t=BROWSE&pf_rd_i=12508

https://www.amazon.com/Illustrated-Mahabharata-Definitive-Guide-Greatest/dp/1465462910/ref=sr_1_2?dchild=1&hvadid=7861513442

6558&hvbmt=bp&hvdev=c&hvqmt=p&keywords=mahabharata&qid=1617393441&sr=8-2

The Nazi Time Machine

https://www.express.co.uk/news/weird/918594/the-nazi-bell-ufo-secret-third-reich-technology-theory-hoax-red-mercury-roswell-incident

https://en.wikipedia.org/wiki/Kecksburg_UFO_incident

https://en.wikipedia.org/wiki/Die_Glocke_

The Vril Society and the Flying Machines

http://www.lost-civilizations.net/flying-vehicles-ancient-egypt.html

Hana Reitsch Photo www.imdb.com

Arthur Skorzeny Photo gettyimages-54339797

Henry Ford and the Third Reich

https://www.pbs.org/wgbh/americanexperience/features/henryford-antisemitism/

America and the Third Reich and the Eugenics Movement

https://www.jstor.org/stable/4330522?seq=1

https://www.plannedparenthood.org/files/9214/7612/8734/Sanger_Fact_Sheet_Oct_2016.pdf

Egypt and the Third Reich

https://en.wikipedia.org/wiki/Gamal_Abdel_Nasser

The North America U

http://www.stopthenorthamericanunion.com/

The EU

https://europa.eu/european-union/index_en

www.ingramcontent.com/pod-product-compliance
Lightning Source LLC
Chambersburg PA
CBHW071407070526
44578CB00002B/508